D1498857

Let's Make a
Tally Chart

by Robin Nelson

first step nonfiction

Lerner Publications Company · Minneapolis

The people in Ben's family
are having a cookout.

They are making hot dogs, hamburgers, and chicken.

Ben's job is to find out
what everyone wants to eat.

How can he keep track?

TEAM A	TEAM B
~~IIII~~ ~~IIII~~ ~~IIII~~	~~IIII~~ ~~IIII~~ ~~IIII~~
~~IIII~~ ~~IIII~~ ~~IIII~~	~~IIII~~ ~~IIII~~ ~~IIII~~
~~IIII~~ ~~IIII~~ ~~IIII~~	~~IIII~~ ~~IIII~~ ~~IIII~~
~~IIII~~ ~~IIII~~ ~~IIII~~	~~IIII~~ ~~IIII~~ ~~IIII~~
	~~IIII~~ ~~IIII~~ III

Ben can make a **tally chart.**

Favorite Pets		
Pets	Tallies	Total
Dog	IIII III	8
Cat	IIII	4
Fish	IIII	4
Bird	II	2

A tally chart shows **data**.
Data is information.

Ben makes a list of the foods.

He asks each person what
he or she wants to eat.

Hot Dog |

Hamburger

Chicken

Ben makes a **tally mark** after the food each person wants.

Every fifth tally mark goes across the other four.

Here is the data Ben got.

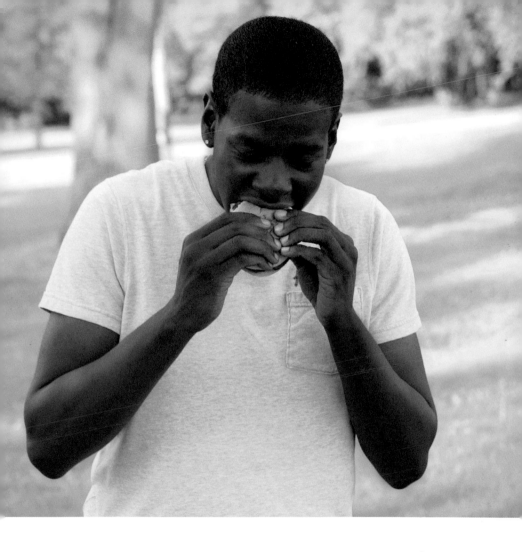

Eight people want
hamburgers.

Five people want hot dogs.

Five people want chicken.

Ben shows his tally chart to his dad.

Time to get the food to the table!

Reading Tally Charts

Ben's aunt, uncle, and two cousins were late to the cookout. Ben asked them what they wanted to eat. He added their answers to his tally chart.

Use Ben's tally chart to answer these questions.

Which foods did the new people choose?

What do the most people want?

How many more people want hamburgers than chicken?

What People Want to Eat

Hot Dog ||||| ||||
= 9

Hamburger ||||| |||
= 8

Chicken |||||
= 5

How to Make a Tally Chart

 Decide what data you want to keep track of.

 Write down the different choices.

 Ask questions to find out people's choices.

 Make tally marks after each choice.

 Add a title.

21

Glossary

 data – information used to make a tally chart

 tally chart – a way to show information that has been counted

 tally mark – a line that stands for one item

Index

The images in this book are used with the permission of: © Larry Dale Gordon/The Image Bank/Getty Images, pp. 2, 16, 17; © Todd Strand/Independent Picture Service, p. 3, 7, 8, 10, 11, 12, 15, 19, 20, 21, 22 (top, bottom); © Larry Dale Gordon/Riser/Getty Images, p. 4; © iStockphoto.com/Tom Young, pp. 5, 9; © iStockphoto.com/Stephen Rees, p. 6, 22 (middle) © Matt Antonio/Dreamstime.com, p. 13; © Yellow Dog Productions/Taxi/Getty Images, p. 14.

Front cover: © Jon Fischer/Independent Picture Service.

Main body text set in ITC Avant Garde Gothic Std Medium 21/25.
Typeface provided by Adobe Systems.

Lerner Publications Company
A division of Lerner Publishing Group, Inc.
241 First Avenue North
Minneapolis, MN 55401 U.S.A.

Website address: www.lernerbooks.com

Library of Congress Cataloging-in-Publication Data

Nelson, Robin, 1971–
    Let's make a tally chart / by Robin Nelson.
        p.   cm. — (First step nonfiction—graph it!)
    Includes index.
    ISBN 978–0–7613–8975–0 (lib. bdg. : alk. paper)
    1. Mathematics—Graphic methods—Juvenile literature. 2. Mathematics—Charts, diagrams, etc.—Juvenile literature. 3. Tallies—Juvenile literature. I. Title.
QA40.5.N456 2013
001.4'226—dc23   2011044875

Manufactured in the United States of America
1 – BC – 7/15/12